Give Go
Things I.
Love in Christ,
Dottie M. Reed

The Gospel of John

Interpreted in Verse by Dottie M. Reed

ISBN-10: 1974524353
ISBN-13: 978-1974524358

Thank You, God, for my Bible,
I love so very much;
Through it I learn of Jesus,
Through it I feel Your Touch.
So close to You it takes me,
I feel humble, yet good inside;
To know through the grace of Jesus,
It was for me He died.
The words won't come I want to write,
To express exactly how I feel;
But I know my love for You,
Is certain, secure, and real.
Without Your love, where would we be?
—Nothing to live for each day;
Your forgiveness has made me know,
I want to live in a better way.
Thank You for helping me complete,
This writing, from Your Gospel of John;
I hope it will help someone else to know,
Of the wonderful things our Lord has done—

Dottie Reed
June 13, 1984

Dedication

To my loving husband, Joe W. Reed.

Also in memory of my brother, Joseph H Mitchell.

Acknowledgements

First I must thank my Lord and Savior Jesus Christ for making my life complete.

Thanks to my husband of 64 years, Joe W. Reed, who told me to "Go for it!" Thanks for the inspiration showered on me from our two children, four grandchildren, two great grandchildren, and all my family, with a very special thanks reserved for my dear cousin, Bonnie Zandt, for her steadfast support.

Thanks also for the encouragement provided by my dear friends in the Living Faith Sunday School Class, including Teacher Faye Bailey, the Delta Amateur Writers, Photographers, and Artists (DAWPA), Pastor Brad Beckwith, and Dr. Macklyn Hubbell and his wife, Bet.

I also extend my enduring gratitude to Margaret Frisbee, who kindly contributed her typing skills to the project.

Finally, I wish to offer a heart-felt thanks to artist and writer Steven Hubbell, whose considerable self-publishing skills allowed me to bring this book to fruition and whose cover art design tenderly expresses my vision of Christ's last moments as he instructed the "disciple whom He loved" (John 19:26-27).

Oh God, I feel so near You,
As I read Your Word each day,
And when I beg Your forgiveness
As I bow my head to pray.
Please give me strength to keep You near
As troubling thoughts creep in
My mind to push the good ones out
And fill it full of sin,
Then when a sinful thought arises
And I wonder what to do....
I ask myself if I do this thing...
How would I explain to You?
And there You are, all the time
Knowing the true nature of my thought,
You're always there to remind me,
It's my life Christ's blood has bought!
How can I ever thank You Lord,
For being so patient with me?
I thank You for Your loving heart
As You try to make me see,
You gave me knowledge of right and wrong
And a conscience to keep me straight.
Why can't I do as You want me to,
Instead of wishing ...when it is too late!
How can I ever thank You God,
For being so patient with me?
I know without asking what would please You
It's be who You would want me to be.

Author's Note...

I pray that as you read this book, you will keep your Bible near at hand so you can search deeper and compare my verses to the precious source, the Word of God, which inspired this labor of love.

> "For even that which was made glorious had no glory in this respect, by reason of the glory that excelleth."
>
> 2 Corinthians 3:10

Table of Contents

Chapter I

(1) Before anything else there was Christ,
He is God, and has always been alive;
He created everything there is,
Without Him nothing could survive.
Eternal life is in Him,
And to mankind He gives light;
Darkness can never extinguish it,
It shines eternally through the night.

(6) God sent John the Baptist,
To identify and witness this fact;
John knew he was not the light,
But, his prophecy was exact.
Although God made the world,
He wasn't recognized when He came;
Only a few would trust Him,
And believe He and Christ are the same.

(14) So Christ became a human,
He told us of God's love;
Some of us have seen His glory,
Through the Son of our Father above.
John pointed out to the people,
Saying, "He is much greater than I;
He existed long before me,
He gives us blessings from on high."
(17) "Moses gave us only the law,
With justice and rigid demands;
While Jesus brings us loving mercy,
He is the only one who can."
The Jewish leaders questioned John,
Of who He was and whence He came;
"I am a voice from the wilderness," said John,
"My prophecy and Isaiah's are the same.
(26) I merely baptize with water,
But in this crowd is One you've never met;
He'll soon begin His ministry among you,
To be His slave, I'm not even fit."

(29) The next day, John saw Jesus,
He was coming his way;
"Behold, the Lamb of God," said John,
"Who takes the world's sin away.
When God sent me to baptize,"
John continued to attest;
(33) "He said I'd see the Holy Spirit descend,
And on someone rest.
He is the Son of God,
I'm here to testify;
He baptizes with the Holy Spirit,
It's true; I'll tell you why."
(32) "I saw the Holy Spirit,
Descend from Heaven above;
He rested on the shoulder of Jesus,
He was in the form of a dove."
The following day, John was standing,
With two disciples there;
Down the road walked Jesus,
"See, the Lamb of God!" John declared.

(37) Then the two disciples left John,
They followed Jesus with something to give;
What do you want? said Jesus,
"Sir," they replied, "Where do you live?"
Come and see, said Jesus,
As He spoke one to the other;
One of these men was Andrew,
Simon Peter's brother.
They stayed with Him til evening,
Then Andrew went down the street;
He found Peter and told him there,
(41) "It's the Messiah, I want you to meet!"
Andrew brought Peter to Jesus,
Jesus looked at him with much intent;
Then He said, *You will be called Peter, the Rock.*
And the next day to Galilee, they went.
There Jesus found Philip,
And said, *You, come with Me.*
Then Philip found Nathanael and told him,
"He's the Messiah, come and see!"

As they approached, Jesus said,

Here comes a true son of Israel.

(48) *You were under a fig tree*

Before Philip found you, Jesus did confide;

"And you are truly the Son of God,

The King of Israel!" Nathanael replied.

Jesus asked, *Do you believe,*

Because I saw you under the tree?

You will see more proof than this,

As God's angels come forth to Me!

Chapter II

Two days later there was a wedding,
At Cana, in Galilee;
(2) Jesus, His disciples and His mother,
Were invited to the festivity.
During the afternoon
They ran out of the supply of wine;
Mary went to Jesus for help,
Not now, He said, *It's not my time.*
But His mother told the servants,
"Do as Jesus asks," (knowing Him);
He told them, *Fill the six stone pots*
With water to the brim
Now dip some out and take it
To the toastmaster as he dines;
The toastmaster drank, but he knew not,
(9) From water, had come the wine.

"Call the bridegroom here!" he said,
"You are different from most;
You saved the best wine 'til the last,
You are a wonderful host!"

(11) This miracle at Cana,
In that certain hour;
Was Jesus' first demonstration
Of "His Heaven sent" power,
Jesus then went to Jerusalem
To observe the Passover law;
There in the temple area,
He was disturbed by what He saw.
He saw merchants selling cattle,
Sheep and dove for sacrifice;
Money changers behind their counters,
Jesus saw every vice!
He made a whip of rope
And drove them out in haste;
He told them, *This is My Father's house,*
It's not a market place!

Then His disciples remembered.
From the Scripture this prophecy;
(17) "Concern I have for God's house,
Will be the undoing of Me."
"By what right do you order them out?"
The Jewish leaders demanded;
"You must show us a miracle,
If this is what God commanded."
(19) *All right*, said Jesus,
This is the miracle I will do;
Destroy this temple and in three days,
I will raise it up for you!
The Jewish leaders scoffed at Jesus,
Saying, "To build this temple took 46 years;
And you can raise it in 3 days?"
They couldn't believe their ears.
But the temple Jesus spoke of
Was His body brought to life again;
His disciples remembered this prophecy,
When the risen Jesus, appeared as a Man.

Many people believed on Him,

Because of the miracles Jesus wrought;

But Jesus knew the hearts of men,

As they changed from what they sought.

Chapter III

A man named Nicodemus,
(1) Was a religious leader of the Jews;
One night under the cover of darkness,
Sought Jesus for an interview.
"Sir," he said, "We all know,
God has sent you to teach the Truth;
Everyone surely agrees,
Your miracles are enough proof."
Jesus replied to Nicodemus,
(5) *I'll tell you this with all earnestness I can*;
You'll never enter the Kingdom of God,
Unless you're born again.
"Born again?" said Nicodemus,
He just didn't understand;
"How can I re-enter my mother's womb,
And then be born again?"

Jesus replied, *Unless you're born of water,*

And of the Spirit, too;

You cannot enter the Kingdom of God,

What I say is true.

Just as you hear the wind,

But can't tell where it comes or goes;

(8) *So it is with the Spirit,*

Whom He chooses next, no one knows."

Jesus continued telling him,

Knowing he didn't understand;

Only I, the Messiah, have come to earth,

And will return to Heaven again.

As Moses in the wilderness,

Lifted the serpent on a pole;

So must I be lifted up,

In order to save your soul.

(16) *For God so loved the world,*

He sent His only Son;

So anyone who believes on Him,

Eternal life He'll give that one.

God sent His Son into the world,
To save and not condemn;
And those who trust and truly believe,
Will live forever with Him.
Those who do not trust,
Have already been tried and convicted;
Their sentence based on the fact,
God's only Son was rejected.
(20) *The light from Heaven beams,*
On those whose deeds are right;
The evil hides in darkness,
In fear of the shining light."
Jesus went on to Judea,
(23) John the Baptist was in Aenon;
Someone argued with John's disciples,
That Jesus was the better one.
Then John's disciples came to him,
Disturbed at what they heard;
Their followers were going to Jesus,
To hear Him preach the Word.

(27) "God in Heaven appointed my work,"
John replied to questions they asked;
"I must go to prepare the way,
For the Messiah, that is my task.
He is the main attraction,
I shall rejoice at His success;
(30) He shall become greater and greater,
I will become less and less.
He has come from Heaven,
And I am of the earth;
(34) He speaks God's words, He was sent by God,
He is God's Son by birth.
The Holy Spirit is in Him,
God has given Him everything;
For those who believe and trust Him,
Eternal life He will bring."

Chapter IV

On the road through Samaria,

(6) Jesus stopped at Jacob's well;

He was tired and thirsty,

(As the Bible will tell.)

His disciples had gone for food,

(7) A Samaritan woman came by;

Jesus asked her for a drink,

She was surprised, and wondered, "Why?"

She was a Samaritan,

He was a Jew—

They hated each other,

This everyone knew.

(10) *If you only knew who I am*, said Jesus,

And about the wonderful gift God has for you;

You would ask me for living water,

No other water would do.

(11) "You don't have a bucket,
You don't even have a rope;
Is your water better than this,
In Jacob's well?" she spoke.
The water I give, Jesus said,
Comes from a perpetual spring within;
If you will only drink from it,
You'll never thirst again.
"Please Sir," she answered,
"Give me this water of which you tell;
I'll never be thirsty again,
And won't have to come to this well."

(16) *Go and get your husband*, said Jesus,
And He told her of things she had done before;
Not fully understanding this,
She questioned Him some more.

(19) "You must be a prophet,
You know the things I do;
But why is Jerusalem the only place,
To worship, for a Jew?"

(21) *The time is coming,* Jesus answered,
When we shall no longer care;
The important thing to realize,
It's how we worship—not where.
For God is the Holy Spirit,
We need His help, to worship as we should;
He wants this kind of worship from us,
But you Samaritans have never understood.

(25) The woman answered, "One thing is plain to see,
The Messiah will come one day;
And everything
Will be explained to me."
Then Jesus told her, *I am the Messiah.*

(27) At that the disciples arrived;
To see Him speaking to a Samaritan woman,
They wondered and were surprised.

(28) Then the woman left the well,
And back to the village she ran;
"Can this really be the Messiah?" she cried,
And told the people "Come and meet this Man!"

(31) Meanwhile, the disciples
Were urging Jesus to eat;
No, said Jesus, *I have some food,*
(But it wasn't meat.)
"Who brought this food?" they answered,
And seeing none, they thought 'twas odd;
(34) Jesus told them, *My nourishment comes,*
From doing the will of God.
Do you think the work of harvesting,
Comes only at summer's end;
Look around at the fields of human souls,
That are ripe for us to win.
(36) *The reaper will receive good wages,*
As he harvests in any weather;
What joys await in Heaven,
For the sower and reaper together!
Many from the village came,
Because of the woman's words;
Jesus stayed in the village two days,
(42) Many believed just because they heard.

(43) Traveling on, He went to Galilee,
The time of day was near one;
(47) A man from Capernaum found Jesus,
And wanted Him to heal his son.
(50) Jesus told him, *Go home,*
Your dying son is well.
The man started home and on his way,
His servants met him with glad news to tell!
"Your son has recovered!" they cried,
The man asked what time it began'
(52) "Yesterday at one o'clock," they answered,
The man started to believe and understand.
Jesus is the Messiah!
The man and his household believed;
(54) This was Jesus' second miracle,
After coming to Galilee.

Chapter V

Crowds of sick—
(3) Blind and lame;
Waited at Bethesda,
While Jesus came.
An angel from the Lord,
Appeared from time to time;
The people waited on the platform,
Looking for a sign
Of a disturbance in the water,
And His presence they could feel;
The first one in the water,
Was the one the Lord would heal.
One of the men lying there,
(5) Had been sick for thirty-eight years;
Wouldn't you like to get well? Jesus asked,
(For He knew of all his fears.)

(7) "I can't," said the man,
"I have no one to help me in;
It's too late when I get there,
Another has already been."
Rise, take up your bed and walk.
Are the words that Jesus said;
Instantly the man was healed,
And walked carrying his bed!
But 'twas on the Sabbath Day,
That this miracle was done;
The Jewish leaders objected,
And they questioned this certain one.
"You can't work on the Sabbath,
(10) It's illegal to carry that mat!"
"I was told to by the Man who healed me," he answered.
They demanded, "Who told you that?"
The man said he didn't know,
And he knew not where Jesus had gone;
(14) Jesus found him later in the Temple,
And there Jesus' name was made known.

Jesus told the man:
Go and sin no more,
Or something worse may happen to you,
Worse than ever before.

(15) The man found the Jewish leaders,
And told them Jesus made him well;
The Jewish leaders then sought to kill Him,
Rather than believe what He had to tell:

(19) *The Son is as the Father,*
The Father as the Son;
The Son only knows and sees to do,
The things His Father has done.
From the miracle of healing this man,
To raising one from the dead;
My Father leaves sins' judgment to Me,
Are the words that Jesus said.

(25) *I say the Day is coming,*
When the dead in their graves shall rise;
Those who have done good to eternal life,
The evil, judgment through God's eyes.

The claims I make are not believed,
(32) *Though John the Baptist says they're true;*
But the greatest witness I have for me,
Are the miracles that I do.
(39) *You believe eternal life,*
Is in the scriptures that you read;
Yet—now you won't come to me,
And I'm the only scripture you need.
You don't have God's love in you,
Though the scripture you know so well;
You won't honor Me, God's Son,
Nor believe what I have to tell.
Moses is your accuser,
(45) *He is the one who wrote of Me;*
You set your hopes upon the law,
But you won't believe the things you see.

Chapter VI

After this Jesus crossed,
(1) The Sea of Galilee;
Great crowds of people followed,
His miracles they wanted to see.
Jesus went higher into the hills,
Where He could not be reached;
He took the disciples with Him,
He needed some time to teach.
But the great crowds followed,
Searching for Him so high
Jesus knew they would be hungry,
And needed some bread to buy.
(9) "There's a lad here, with five loaves,
And two fish," Disciple Andrew spoke'
"But what good would that do,
With five thousand hungry folk?"

(10) Jesus told the people to sit, give thanks,
He fed them, fine as they had tasted;
Now gather up the scraps, He said,
So nothing there was wasted.

(15) The people wanted Him to be their King,
When they'd realized the miracle He'd done;
And Jesus— (knowing this),
Went higher into the mountains alone.

(16) That evening His disciples
Went to the shore to wait;
Jesus hadn't come down,
They were worried because He was late.

(17) Darkness fell—
They got into the boat;
A storm swept down,
They could hardly stay afloat.
They rowed and rowed,
The wind blew harder;

(19) Then suddenly they saw Jesus,
Walking on the water!

The disciples were terrified,
And Jesus raised His hand;
Don't be afraid, He said,
And immediately they were at land.
The crowds now searched for Jesus,
He'd gone they knew not where;
They rowed across the lake,
And found Him speaking there.
Saying: *Seek eternal life,*
That I the Messiah can give;
God has sent Me for this purpose,
That you shall forever live.
"Show us more miracles," they replied,
"And give us free bread every day;
Moses fed our fathers,
Is what the scriptures say!"
Moses didn't feed them,
My Father did, Jesus said;
Now He sends Me to you,
I am the only True Bread.

"Give us that bread!" they answered,
"Every day of our lives!"
Accept Me as that Bread, said Jesus,
And that last day you shall rise.

(36) *Some of you will not believe,*
Though you've seen the things I've done;
But those my Father gives Me,
I will lose not one.

(41) The Jews murmured against Him,
When they heard His claim,
"We know His father and mother," they said,
We know from whence He came!"
Jesus replied to them,
(Knowing what they said),

(44) *The ones my Father draws to Me,*
I will raise from the dead!
How earnestly I tell you this,
Believe on Me and live;
I was sent to redeem humanity,
The Bread is my flesh I give.

(52) Then the Jews gave argument
Not knowing what He meant;
Jesus tried to tell them again,
Tell them why he was sent.
Unless you eat of my flesh, said Jesus,
And drink of the blood therein;
You cannot have eternal life,"
This He repeated again.

(60) Even His disciples said,
"This is too hard to understand,"
And Jesus knowingly answered,
You shall see Me go to Heaven again.
Some of you don't believe me,
But what I say is true.

(66) Many disciples deserted Him now,
He asked the twelve, *Are you going, too*?
"Master, to whom shall we go?" said, Peter,
"We believe You are God's Son;
You can give eternal life,
You are the only One."

And Jesus said, *I chose you twelve,*

But the devil is in a certain one.

(71) He was then speaking of Judas,

Simon Iscariot's son.

Chapter VII

(1) Jesus went to Galilee,
Going from town to town;
The Jewish leaders were plotting His death,
(In Judea He would be found.)
But soon it was time for the Tabernacle ceremonies,
An annual Jewish holiday;
The celebration was in Judea,
(3) His own brothers were heard to say,
"You must go to Judea,
And show your miracles there;
You can't be famous when you hide like this!"
(Even His own brothers didn't believe or care.)
Jesus told them it wasn't time for Him,
But none cared if they went or when;
(7) *The world doesn't hate you, but it does me,*
For I accuse it of evil and sin.

After His brothers left, then Jesus went
(10) Staying out of the public eye;
He heard lots of discussion about himself,
Of when He had come and why.
Midway through the festival,
In the Temple, Jesus began to preach;
The Jewish leaders were surprised He knew so much,
And murmured as He continued to teach.
(16) So Jesus told them, *What I say,*
Are the thoughts that God instills;
And the only ones who truly know this,
Are those who do His will.
None of you obey the law,
Why kill Me for the same;
I healed a man on the Sabbath,
Made him well because he was lame.
Jesus' preaching in the Temple,
Caused much confusion and talk;
(25) "Wasn't He the man they wanted to kill,
Yet—He was free to walk.

Could He really be the Messiah?

No! The Messiah would just appear;

We know where this Man was born,

But—What is He doing here?"

(28) So Jesus in a sermon answered,

Yes, you know where I was born and raised;

But, I represent One you do not know,

And He is truth, be praised.

I know Him because I was with Him,

He was the One that sent Me to you.

The Jewish leaders then wanted to seize Him,

But the time wasn't right, Jesus knew.

Many of the crowds in the Temple believed,

That He was truly God's Son;

(31) "What miracles," they said, "Can the Messiah do,

That this Man hasn't done?"

The crowds were going to Jesus,

The Pharisees were beginning to fret;

They sent officers to arrest Him,

But Jesus told them, *Not yet.*

(33) *I am here for a little while,*
Then from the One, I came, I shall go;
You will search for Me, but can't come to Me,
For where I am you won't know.
This puzzled the Jewish leaders,
They wondered, but couldn't understand;
"Maybe He was going as a missionary
To Jews or Gentiles, in other lands."
At the climax of the holidays,
Jesus stood where all could see;
(37) Then He shouted to the people,
If you are thirsty, come to Me!
For the river of Living Water,
To the believers shall be given!
(He was speaking of the Holy Spirit they'd receive,
When He returned to Heaven.)
When the crowds heard Him say this,
(40) Indecision filled the air;
"He is the prophet that comes,
Before the Messiah," some declared.

(41) Others said, "He is the Messiah,
You just wait and see!"
Others said, "He cannot be,
He came from Galilee!"
The scriptures clearly state,
The Messiah will be of David's royal line;"
(Since David was born in Bethlehem,)
(43) The crowd was divided at that time.
Some wanted Him arrested,
But not one would take the task;
The Temple police were questioned,
By the Pharisees, and were asked:
"Why didn't you arrest Him?
And bring Him in, we've told you o'er!"
(46) "He says such wonderful things," they answered,
"Things we've never heard before."
"So you're like the stupid crowds,
And you've been led astray!
(49) We Pharisees and leaders don't believe it,
A curse on you, anyway!"

Then Nicodemus spoke up,

(51) "Can we convict a man not tried?"

"No prophet will come from Galilee,

Search the scripture!" they replied.

Then the meeting broke up,

And each to his home they started;

There were mixed emotions,

In their hearts, as they departed.

Chapter VIII

(1) Jesus returned to the Mount of Olives
The next day, back to the Temple He walked;
When He was seen, a crowd soon gathered,
And Jesus sat down and talked.
(3) The Jewish leaders brought forth a woman,
Caught in the act of sin;
They placed her in front of the staring crowd
And questioned Jesus again.
They told Jesus she was caught in adultery,
And Moses' law said she was to die;
(6) They were trying to trap Jesus,
Jesus knew all this, and why.
Jesus stooped to the ground,
And with His finger wrote in the dust;
They kept demanding an answer,
And answer them He must!

(7) Jesus stood up and told them,
All right, hurl the stones 'til she dies;
He who has never sinned, throw the first.
Then He watched their eyes.
Then there on the ground, He continued to write,
(9) But the Jewish leaders, one by one, slipped away;
'Til only Jesus and the woman were left,
In front of the crowd that day.
Then Jesus stood up and asked her,
(10) *Where are you accusers now*?
Didn't even one condemn you?
"No, Sir," she said, as her head began to bow.
And Jesus said, *Nor* I,
Go and sin no more.
Then He started to talk to the people again,
Telling them things He had told them before.
(12) *I am the Light of the World*, He continued,
Follow Me, through the darkness I'll lead;
Living Light will flood your path.
Then from the crowd called a Pharisee.

(13) "You're boasting and lying!" He said,
But Jesus continued to speak;
The claims I make of myself are true.
I know the things you seek.
You pass judgement without knowing the fate,
I am not judging you now;
But if I were I would be right,
For my Father is telling me how.
Your laws say if two agree,
Then their witness is accepted as fact;
Well, I am one witness, My Father, the other,
And what I say is exact.
"Who is your father?" they replied,
(19) And what Jesus answered was true;
You don't know Me, then you don't know Him
If you knew Me, you would know Him, too.
I'm going away and you will search for me,
But you cannot come where I go;
You'll die in your sins. Jesus said,
Then questions, went to and fro.

(22) "What does He mean? Where is He going?
Is He planning suicide?"
The Jewish leaders couldn't comprehend,
About Him, they couldn't decide.
You are of this world below,
I am the Son of God on high;
Unless you believe I am the Messiah,
Then you will surely die.
(25) "Tell us who you are!" they demanded,
And Jesus told them again;
I do what I'm told by the One who sent me,
But the people still didn't understand.
Jesus said, *When you've killed the Messiah,*
Then you will realize I am He;
I speak the words God tells me to,
He has not deserted Me.
When some of the Jewish leaders heard this,
(30) They believed the Messiah was He;
Live as I tell you, Jesus said,
And the truth shall set you free.

(33) "But we are descendants of Abraham," they said,
"We have never been anyone's slave!"
What do you mean when you say 'set free?'
And they listened to the answer Jesus gave.
You are truly slaves—of sin—,
Every single one —;
And slaves you know, have no rights,
(36) *Unless they're set free by the Son.*
Yes, I realize you are Abraham's descendants,
But with my message some won't agree;
I am telling you what I saw with my Father,
Still yet—some want to kill me.
(39) "Abraham is our father," they declared.
The crowd just wouldn't be still;
No, said Jesus, *He wouldn't act like you,*
In hearing truth, he wouldn't kill.
"Then God is our true Father," they said,
And Jesus made His answer known;
(42) *If that were so, then you would love me,*
For I am not here on my own.

God has sent me here to earth,

(43) *Why can't you understand?*

It is because you are sons of the devil,

You love the evils of his hand.

He was a murderer from the beginning,

And the father of every lie;

So when I tell you the truth you can't believe it,

You are his children, that's why!

Can you accuse Me of a single sin?

You won't believe the truth you've heard;

If you were truly children of God

You would gladly hear His word!

This made the Jewish leaders angrier,

And they wouldn't let it rest;

"Samaritan, foreigner, devil!", they yelled,

(52) "By a demon you are possessed!"

No, said Jesus, *That is not true,*

I honor my Father on High;

With all earnestness, I tell you again,

Obey me, and you shall never die.

"Now we know you're possessed," they said,
"Even Abraham and the other prophets died;
You think you're greater than Abraham?
Who are you, and why have you lied?"
You claim my Father as your God, said Jesus,
(55) *But you do not know Him as I do;*
I know Him, and I fully obey Him,
If I said otherwise, I'd be a liar as you.
(56) *Your father, Abraham knew I was coming,*
He rejoiced and was truly glad.
The Jewish leaders mocked Jesus,
Then they began to get mad.
"Sure, you've seen Abraham," they said,
"You aren't even fifty years old!"
(58) *I existed even before Abraham was born,*
Is the truth that Jesus told.
At that point the Jewish leaders,
Picked up stones to throw;
Jesus was hidden, and walked right past,
Where He was they didn't know.

Chapter IX

The disciples had a question for Jesus,

As they walked about this day;

(1) They saw a man, blind from birth,

And asked Jesus why it happened that way.

"Is it the result of his own sin,

Or something his parents had done?"

Neither, said Jesus, *But to demonstrate God's power*

I must quickly give light to this one.

(6) Jesus spat on the ground, made mud from the spittle,

Smoothed the mud o'er the blind man's eyes;

He told him, *Go wash in the Pool of Siloam*,

The man did without asking why.

When he came back, people who knew him,

Were amazed that he could see;

"Are you the same fellow, the blind beggar,

Tell us how this can be?"

Then the man told them what Jesus had done,
(But this occurred on the Sabbath Day;)
(13) They took him to the Pharisees, who listened to his story,
And questioned him in every way.
Opinions were split over who Jesus was,
When the story was repeated again;
"He's not from God, He works on the Sabbath,
But can a sinner do the miracles of this Man?"
(17) The Pharisees questioned the man,
Who did he think Jesus was?
"I think He must be a prophet," he answered,
"A prophet sent from God."
Then they questioned his parents,
If he was really their son;
Was he truly born blind,
Yet he could see, how then was this done?
(20) "He is our son," they answered in fear,
"He was born blind, but now he can see;
But, we don't know what happened to him,
Or how this came to be."

Then they called the man again,
Before them the second time;
"Give the glory to God," they told him,
Jesus is evil, we find."
"I know not whether he's good or bad,
But I know what happened to me;
For I do know this," the man replied,
(25) "I was blind but now I can see!"
The Pharisees cursed and called him names,
As he defended Jesus that day;
"Jesus couldn't have made me see,
If God hadn't showed Him the way!
(32) There has never been anyone else,
That could heal a person born blind;
You know nothing of this Man,
Because it's evil you try to find."
The angry Pharisees wouldn't listen,
And threw him out the door;
Jesus heard what happened, sought him out,
And talked to him some more.

Do you believe in the Messiah?
He asked, when the man was found;
(36) "Who is He, Sir, for I want to,"
The man answered looking around.
You have seen Him, said Jesus,
He is now speaking to you!
(38) "Yes, Lord, I believe," the man said,
And worshiped Jesus anew.
To those who are spiritually blind,
Jesus said, *I have come to give Sight*
And to show those, who think they see,
They've never seen the Light.
"Are you saying we are blind?"
Asked the Pharisees when they heard;
If you were blind you wouldn't be guilty,
Was Jesus' answer to their words.
Your guilt remains because you claim,
To know what you are doing.
The Pharisees discussed this—
And Jesus watched them, —knowing.

Chapter X

The Good Shepherd comes through the gate,

When He comes to care for His sheep;

(Anyone else sneaking over the wall,

Must surely be a thief).

(3) *The gate keeper opens the gate for Him,*

And the sheep then hear His voice;

He calls His own by name and leads them out,

They follow Him by choice.

(6) Jesus gave this illustration,

But people knew not what He meant;

So as He then explained to them,

They listened with much intent.

(8) *All others before Me were thieves and robbers,*

For I am the Gate for the sheep;

The sheep did not listen to them,

Those coming through Me, I shall keep.

They will be saved and find green pastures,

The thief's purpose is to destroy and kill;

My purpose is to give life fully,

The true sheep will be fulfilled.

A hired man runs, when the wolf comes,

He has no real concern for his sheep;

His flock is scattered, he doesn't care,

For they are not his to keep.

(14) *I am the Good Shepherd, I know my sheep,*

I lay down my life for them;

My Father knows Me, as I know my Father,

As My sheep know Me, I know Him.

I have other sheep, to them I call,

They are in another fold;

I will bring them in so there will be one flock,

They will come to Me when they're told.

(17) *My Father loves Me, because I lay down My life,*

That I may have it back again;

I lay down My life voluntarily,

No one can kill Me, unless I say they can.

(19) When Jesus said these things, arguments started,
Jewish leaders were divided again;
Some said He's a demon, others said He's crazy,
Yet – He's opened the eyes of blind men.

(23) Jesus was in the Temple one day,
Walking through Solomon's Hall;
The Jewish leaders surrounded Him there,
"Tell us who you are!" they called.
I have already told you, Jesus answered,
But you don't believe why I came;
Yet, the proof is in the miracles I do,
In my Father's name.
You are not part of my flock,
They know Me and I know My sheep;
They follow Me to eternal life,
My Father gave them for Me to keep.
No one can snatch them away from Me,
This My Father has done;
He is more powerful than anyone else,
(30) *I and the Father are One.*

(31) Then again the Jewish leaders,
Were angered and wanted to kill;
Why are you killing Me? said Jesus,
I've done only good at God's will.
They replied, "Not for good works,
But for words of blasphemy;
Here you are—a mean man
Declaring yourself a God to be!"
Jesus answered, *Your own law says men are gods,*
And your scriptures can't be untrue;
If you don't believe the words I say,
(38) *Believe God's miracles that I do.*
Once again they started to arrest Him,
But He walked away at will:
He went to stay near the Jordan River,
And men followed Him, still.
"John didn't do miracles," they remarked,
"But his predictions concerning Jesus are true."
Many decided, "He is the Messiah,"
And who they were, Jesus knew.

Chapter XI

Now Jesus' friend named Lazarus,
Who lived in Bethany town;
(With his sisters, Martha and Mary,)
Was sick to death, they found.

(3) The sisters sent Jesus a message,
Saying, "Your friend Lazarus is very sick;
We know that you can heal him"
(They hoped He would come quick.)
Jesus received the message,
And He knew the reason why;
For God would receive the glory,
And Lazarus would not die.
Although Jesus was very fond of them,
He made no move to go;
Until the next two days had passed,
Seemingly very slow.

Let us go to Judea, said Jesus.

My friends have need of Me;

But His disciples objected,

There, His life was in jeopardy.

Jesus replied to their objection,

Saying, *It is safe to walk by day;*

Only at night is there any danger,

For in the dark you can't see the way.

(11) *Our friend Lazarus has gone to sleep,*

But I will go wake him now.

The disciples thought Lazarus was resting,

And getting better somehow.

But Jesus told them plainly,

Lazarus is dead!

And I'm glad I wasn't there

For it will help you believe the things I've said.

(16) "Let us go with Him" said Thomas, the twin,

To his fellow disciples that day;

"If He dies, we'll die with Him,"

They'd go with Him all the way.

(19) Now, many of the Jewish leaders,
Were at Mary and Martha's home;
Consoling them on the loss of their brother,
For they were all alone.
Lazarus had been in his tomb four days,
When Mary and Martha were told
That Jesus and His disciples,
Were coming down the road.
Martha ran to meet them,
Mary stayed at home;
"Sir, if you had been there," said Martha,
"My brother would not be gone!"
"Even now it's too late,
But if you would only ask;
God to bring him back to life— "
She challenged Jesus to the task.
Your brother will come to life again,
She heard Jesus say;
"Yes, —when everyone else does," she answered,
"On Resurrection Day."

(25) *I am the One*, said Jesus,
Who raises the dead, and life I give;
Anyone who believes on Me,
Tho' he dies—he shall live.
Do you believe this, Martha?
Jesus plainly stated;
"Yes," said Martha, "I believe,
You're the Messiah we've so long awaited."
Martha left Him and returned—
(28) To Mary, and called her aside;
"He is here," she told her sister,
"And wants to see you!" she cried.
Mary left at once—
And Jewish leaders saw her go;
They thought she was going to Lazarus' tomb,
And followed her to know,
When Mary arrived where Jesus was,
She fell down at His feet;
"Sir, if you'd been here, he'd be alive!"
And Jesus watched her weep.

He then saw the Jewish leaders,
Wailing with her as she mourned;
He was deeply troubled,
With indignation and with scorn.

(34) *Where is he buried*? asked Jesus,
They answered, "Come and see;"
Jesus wept.
For—all knowing—was He.
In the conversations,
As they were walking to the grave;
Some said, "He healed a blind man,
Yet Lazarus, He couldn't save."
Listening, Jesus was moved with anger,
As He had been before;
And when they reached the tomb,
There was a stone across the door.
Roll the stone aside, said Jesus,
A miracle from God you now shall see;

(41) Then Jesus looked up to Heaven and said,
Thank you God for hearing Me.

(43) Then He shouted, *Lazarus, come forth*!
And there bound in grave cloth from head to toe;
Lazarus came forth, alive from the grave,
Jesus said, *Unwrap him and let him go.*

(45) At last, many of the Jewish leaders,
Who saw Lazarus come hence;
Believed Jesus was the Son of God,
Yet others still weren't convinced.
And they told the chief priests and Pharisees,
Then a special meeting convened;
To decide what to do about Jesus,
And the miracles they had seen.
"If we let Him alone," they said,
"The Roman army shall come;
Because the nation will follow Him,
They'll kill us every one."

(49) The High Priest named Caiaphas,
Then gave a statement so bold;
Little did he know—
It was what Jesus had foretold.

(50) "Let a nation perish—No!
For the people, let this one man die!"
(Caiaphas was inspired to say this,
To fulfill God's plans on High.)
In the prediction that Jesus' death,
Be for God's children everywhere;
Not just for Israel alone,
To know God's eminent care.

(54) Jesus now stopped His public ministry,
And left Jerusalem;
Then stayed with His disciples
In the village of Ephraim.
As the Passover drew near,
To Jerusalem people came;
Early to the Temple for cleansing,
Where all heard Jesus' name.
"Will He come to Passover?"
"It's Him we want to see."
"What do you think of the things He does,
And says of what is to be?"

(57) Meanwhile, a proclamation was made,
By the Priests and Pharisees;
That Jesus would be under arrest,
When He was seen, He would be seized!

Chapter XII

Six days before the Passover,
To Bethany Jesus came;
There at the house of Lazarus,
Was prepared a banquet in Jesus' name.
(2) Martha served the table,
Lazarus sat with Him there;
Mary anointed His feet with perfume
And wiped them with her hair.
The house was filled with fragrance,
Then Judas Iscariot spoke;
(5) "That perfume should have been sold,
The money given to poor folk."
(Not that he cared for the poor,
That really was not his belief;
He often took money from the disciples' fund,
Truly in his heart he's a thief.)

(7) Jesus replied, *Let her alone*
For my burial, she did it to prepare;
I won't be with you very long,
But the poor will always be there.
Jesus had arrived!
The news spread throughout the town;
People flocked to see Him,
At Lazarus' house, He would be found.
There they would see the Master,
And the man He had raised from the dead;
Then the chief priests decided to kill Lazarus, too,
(11) For because of him, some priests, to Jesus were led.
The next day Jesus came to Jerusalem,
(14) On the back of a donkey He sat;
Fulfilling the prophecy before Him,
(At the time no one realized that.)
The huge crowd of Passover visitors,
Met Him with palm branches held high;
Paying Jesus their homage,
Trusting He was the Messiah.

And those who had seen the miracle,
Of Lazarus' return from the grave;
Told others, and news of the miracle spread,
That Jesus had come to save –
The Pharisees observing the crowds,
Were aggravated and very 'put out';
"We've lost!' they said to each other.
As they began to doubt.

(20) Some Greeks had come for Passover,
And told Philip, 'twas Jesus they wanted to meet;
Philip told Andrew, and together they went,
To ask Jesus, who was preaching in the street.

(23) Jesus replied that the time had come,
When to Heaven's glory He'd return;
I shall die like a kernel of wheat,
(He explained this, hoping they would learn.)
Unless I die, I will be...
—As a single seed alone—
But my death will bring plentiful harvest,
Many lives will be saved when I've gone.

(25) *If you love your life here you will lose it,*

Jesus continued His story;

If you hate your life here you will change it,

And live in eternal Glory.

If these Greeks want to be my disciples,

Tell them to come, they must follow me;

For my servants must be where I am,

And honor, there will also be.

Now, my soul is deeply troubled,

Should I pray, "Father, save me from whence I came?"

But that is the reason for what lies ahead,

To bring honor and glory to your name.

(28) Then a voice from Heaven spoke saying,

I've already done this, I'll do it again.

The crowd heard the voice, and wondered,

If 'twas thunder, or an angel speaking to this Man.

Jesus then told them the voice,

Was spoken for their benefit alone;

It's time for Satan to be cast out,

And Judgment for the world has come.

(32) *I will draw you to Me*, He said,
When I am lifted up high;
He told them this in indication,
Of how He was going to die.
"The Messiah will never die," they said,
As they crowded around Him together;
"Just what Messiah do you speak of,
He's supposed to live forever!"

(35) *My light will shine for a little while*, said Jesus,
Walk in it while you can;
Go where you want before it's too late,
For darkness will cover this land.
Make use of the light,
And light bearers you will be;"
Then Jesus went away and was hidden from them,
In a place they could not see.

(37) But despite the miracles He'd done,
Most of the people would not believe;
Isaiah had predicted this from a vision,
God's miracles they couldn't conceive.

(40) For their hearts were hardened and eyes were closed,
They couldn't receive the feeling;
They could neither see nor understand,
Or turn to Jesus for healing.

(42) However, many of the Jewish leaders believed,
But wouldn't admit it because of fear;
Of being excommunicated from the church,
To them, the praise of men was very dear.
Jesus continued preaching to the crowds,
Telling them of darkness coming soon;
If they did not see God in Him,
The Day of Judgment would be their doom.
Though, He was not sent to judge,
This world, He came to redeem;
The ideas He spoke were God's alone,
Through Jesus, God is seen.

Chapter XIII

(1) Jesus knew on Passover evening,
It was His last night in this land;
The devil had spoken to Judas,
To carry out His plan.
Jesus knew He had come from God,
And to God He would return;
For God had given Him everything,
Jesus knew and could discern.
He got up from the supper table,
Replaced the robe He wore,
A towel, He wrapped around His loins,
(5) Then in a basin, water, He did pour.
Next, He began to wash their feet,
And with the towel wipe them dry;
The disciples didn't understand this,
Then Peter asked Him, "Why?"

Jesus replied, *You don't know now,*
But then, someday you will;
(8) "You'll never wash my feet!" said Peter,
For this, he couldn't be still!
But if I don't, said Jesus,
You can never be a part of me;
Then Simon Peter told Him,
"Wash my hands and head—not just my feet."
(10) *One who has bathed all over*, said Jesus,
Needs only his feet washed, to be entirely clean;
But that's not true of everyone here,
(Meaning the betrayer on the scene.)
(12) After washing their feet, He put on His robe,
And sat down with words to explain;
He wanted them to understand,
Their purpose and what they could attain.
You call me Lord and Master,
You do well to say it, for it's true;
I have given you an example to follow,
Now do—as I have done unto you.

(16) *For a servant isn't greater than His master,*

This point Jesus was stressing;

You know these things, now do them, he said,

That is the path of great blessing.

(18) *I do not say this to all of you,*

For you I chose, I know so well;

One of you will betray me soon,

Fulfilling what the scriptures tell.

By telling you this now, when time has passed,

You'll believe on me even more;

(20) *Anyone welcoming you is welcoming Me,*

And my Father, as I've told you before.

Now Jesus was in great anguish of spirit,

And exclaimed, *Yes, it is true;*

One of you will betray me,

(The disciples now wondering, "Who"?)

John was sitting next to Jesus,

Being His closest friend;

(24) Simon Peter told him to ask Jesus,

"Who was going to turn Him in?"

(26) Jesus answered, *It is the one,*
I honor in this way;
He dipped the bread in sauce, gave it to Judas,
And Judas heard Him say.
Hurry, do it now,
And Judas left Him there;
For Satan had entered into him,
And Judas didn't care.

(28) The others at the table,
Knew not what Jesus meant;
Since Judas was the treasurer,
It could be about money he spent.

(31) As soon as Judas left the room,
Jesus said, *My time has come;*
And God shall receive great praise and glory,
Because of what I have done.

(32) *And God shall give me His own glory,*
The time is near at hand;
For I must go where you cannot come,
So I'm giving you a new command.

It is: Love each other as I love you,

Do this and people will know;

That you are my disciples,

Everywhere you go.

(36) "But Master, where will you go?"

Simon Peter inquired;

You will know later when you come to me,

Jesus lovingly replied.

But Peter asked, "Why can't I come now,

For you, I am ready to die!!"

(38) Jesus said, *Die for Me—No,*

And He looked Peter in the eye.

Feeling compassion for Peter,

Yet giving him this warning;

Three times you will have denied Me,

Before the cock crows in the morning.

Chapter XIV

(1) *Let not your heart be troubled,*

You are trusting God, now trust in Me;

I go to prepare a place for you,

So where I am, you can always be.

I will come for you when I'm ready,

I'd tell you, if this were not true;

You know where I'm going and how to get there,

And Jesus told them what they must do.

"*I am the Way, the Truth, and the Life,*

No one goes to the Father but by Me;

If you know who I am, you know the Father,

When you've seen Me, it's Him you see.

(8) "Philip said, "Sir, show us the Father,

And we will be satisfied;"

Don't you even know who I am,

After all this time? Jesus replied.

Any one who has seen Me has seen the Father,
So why are you asking for Him to see?
Don't you believe I am in the Father,
And the Father is in Me?
The words I say are from my Father,
They are not my own, it's true;
Just believe it because I say it,
Or because of the miracles that I do.

(12) *In solemn truth I tell you this,*
Believe in Me, and do the miracles I've done;
Ask My Father for anything in My name,
And He will do it for I am His Son.

(15) *If you love Me—obey Me,*
And another Comforter shall come;
In the form of the Holy Spirit,
But, He'll be received by only some.
In a while I'll be gone,
But be present with you still;
And the ones of you who love Me,
Shall always do my will.

When I return to life again,
This—you will see;
(20) *I am in My Father,*
And you are in Me.
Because if one loves Me,
He shall always do my will;
My Father will love him,
And to him, I'll be revealed.
I reveal myself to those of you who love Me,
My Father shall love them, too;
We will come to them and live with them,
And they will always know what to do.
I tell you this while I am still with you,
(26) *But later when the Comforter comes;*
He will teach you much, but also remind you,
Of the things I've already said and done.
The peace I give is not the peace of the world,
But the peace of the heart and mind;
I go to My Father, but leave you this peace,
It's like no other peace you will find.

(29) *If you love Me, be happy for Me,*
For I go to the Father, Who's greater than I;
I tell these things before they happen,
So you will believe in Me when I die.
The time is now short, as I speak with you,
The evil prince is coming near by;
He has no power over Me, and I freely do,
To show My love, that My Father requires.

Chapter XV

(1) *I am the true vine and My Father the Gardener,*
You are the branches from Me;
He prunes you back for larger crops,
If you don't produce, you're cut off from Me.
So take care to live in Me, and Me in you,
For a branch can't produce severed from the vine;
You'll have greater strength by the commands I give you,
Obey them and bountiful harvests are thine.
I have loved you as My Father loved Me,
(9) *Abide in My love;*
This means obey Me, as I have obeyed—
My Father in Heaven above.
I tell you this so you'll be filled with My joy,
Yes—your cup will overflow;
And to lay down your life for another,
Is the greatest love you will ever know.

(15) *I no longer call you slaves,*
For in slaves, a master won't confide;
Now you are My friends, proved by the fact,
I've told you everything My Father provides.
You didn't choose Me, the choice was Mine,
And if you go, and do My will;
No matter what you ask the Father in My name,
He will surely give.
I demand that you love each other,
For from this world enough hate you'll receive;
You came out of the world because I chose you,
(18) *The world hates you because you believe.*
Since they persecute Me, they will persecute you,
And in listening, it would be the same;
The people of the world will persecute you,
Because they don't know I came in God's name.
They would not be guilty, if I had not come,
For I spoke and showed them miracles, but then;
They still hate Me, also hating My Father,
Now there is no excuse for their sin.

(23) *Yes, they still hate Me and My Father,*

Even after the miracles they could see;

This fulfilled the prophecy concerning the Messiah,

'Without reason they hated Me'.

(26) *But I will send the Comforter,*

The Holy Spirit, the source of everything true;

He comes from the Father and will tell more about Me,

And you must tell everyone, too.

Chapter XVI

(1) *I have told you these things so you'll be prepared,*
For all that will come to be;
Excommunication and death from people,
Who know not the Father and Me.
And when these things have happened,
You will remember what I foretold;
For now I am going to the One who sent Me,
(6) *And only sorrow in you unfolds.*
It is best for you that I go,
Though none of you wonders why;
The fact of the matter is,
(7) *The Holy Spirit won't come lest I die.*
Yes, the Comforter will come,
For I shall send Him to you;
He will convince the world of its sin,
And what God's goodness can do.

The world's sin is unbelief in Me,

But there is deliverance from sin;

Because, I go to the Father for this purpose,

And one day, I shall come again.

(12) *Oh, there is so much I want to tell you,*

But you can't understand it now;

So the Holy Spirit shall come to guide you,

And to you, Truth, He shall allow.

(14) *He shall bring me honor and glory,*

And forever praise my name;

The Father's glory belongs to me,

For the Father and I are the same.

In just a little while, I'll be gone,

And you will see Me no more;

But then later, you will see Me again,

And your joy will be greater than before.

(18) "Whatever is He saying?"

The disciples asked each other;

Jesus knew their confusion,

And He explained to them further:

This world will greatly rejoice,
Over what is going to happen to Me;
And your own weeping will turn to joy,
When I return, and it's Me you see.
It will be the same joy you'll have,
As a woman giving birth;
The pain will be forgotten,
(22) *Replaced by rapturous joy, that it was worth.*
Yes, you will have sorrow now,
But when I return you will rejoice;
Then ask My Father anything in My name,
And He will fulfill your choice.
You have never done this before,
Because you didn't know;
But when you start asking Him in My name,
(24) *Your cup of joy will overflow.*
Yes, you will go to the Father,
With your petitions in My name;
He will grant them, for He loves you,
(27) *And you believe from Him, I came.*

(28) *Yes, I came from the Father into the world,*
And to My Father I shall return;
Jesus was telling them plainly,
Hoping they would learn.
"Now we understand," said the disciples,
"That You know everything there is to know;
And from this, we believe You came from God,
Here to the earth below."
(31) *Do you finally believe this*? Jesus asked,
But, the time is coming, in fact, it is here;
When you will all be scattered,
Going to your own homes in fear.
You will leave Me alone—
Yet, alone I will not be;
I will have My Father,
For He is always with Me.
I have told you this to give you peace,
As your trials and sorrows unfurl;
(33) *Do not worry—but cheer up,*
For I have overcome the world!

Chapter XVII

(1) When Jesus had finished saying these things,
He looked up to Heaven and said;
Father, the time has come,
To reveal what You have planned ahead.
Reveal the Glory of Your Son,
So He can give it back to You;
He gives eternal life to those you've given Him,
By showing them, the only God that is true.
I brought You glory by doing Your bid,
When You sent Me to this land;
Oh, Father reveal My glory now, in Your presence,
That we shared before the world began.
(6) *I have told these men all about You,*
They were in the world, but You gave them to me;
Actually, they were already Yours,
And now Yours, they will always be.

They have obeyed You—

(7) *And now they understand;*

That everything I have is a gift from You,

And I have passed them Your commands.

They have accepted them and know for certain,

That I came down to earth from You;

And they believe You sent Me, Father,

(10) *So they are Mine and My glory, too.*

Now I am leaving this world,

And leaving them behind;

Keep them in Your care, Holy Father,

For they are of My kind.

They will be united as We,

And none missing, not one;

They were kept safe in Your family,

We only lost—the devil's son.

May they be filled with My joy,

As I come to You in this hour;

They do not fit in this world, Holy Father,

(15) *Oh, keep them safe from Satan's power.*

Teach them Your words of truth,
I send them as You sent Me;
Your words will make them holy and pure,
And I, Myself, will meet their need.

(20) *I am not praying for these alone,*
But also, for future believers who come;
My prayer is that all will be one heart and mind,
Just as You and I are One.
I gave them the glory You gave Me,
The glorious unity of being One as We are;
I in them, You in Me, they understand,
Your love for them is more than par.

(24) *Father, I want them with Me, the ones You give,*
So My glory they can see;
The glory You gave Me before the world began,
Because You have always loved Me.

(25) *Oh righteous Father, the world doesn't know You,*
But I do, and My disciples know from You I stem;
I will continue to reveal Your mighty love through Me,
And We will always be in them.

Chapter XVIII

(1) After saying these things,
Jesus' disciples followed Him;
They crossed the Kidron ravine
To a place well know to them.
For Jesus had gone there many times,
To teach His disciples what to do;
'Twas in a grove of olive trees,
Where Judas the betrayer knew,
At this time, Judas arrived
Accompanied by soldiers and police;
With blazing torches and weapons,
It was Jesus they came to seize.
(4) Jesus was well aware,
Of the events that were coming to pass;
And stepping forward to meet them —
Whom are you seeking? He asked.

"Jesus of Nazareth!"

The group in chorus replied;

(5) *I am He*, said Jesus,

They fell to the ground as they sighed.

Whom are you searching for?

Jesus' question was the same;

"Jesus of Nazareth!" they replied,

Answering Him again.

I told you I am He, said Jesus,

Let the others go free.

(9) Jesus said this to carry out

The telling of His prophecy.

Malchus was the High Priest's servant,

He was standing near;

Simon Peter took a sword,

(10) And slashed off his right ear!

Jesus said to Peter,

Put your sword away;

Shall I not drink from the cup,

That my Father says I may!

(12) Now Jesus was placed under arrest,
And to the High Priest He was sent;
Simon Peter and another disciple,
Followed, as they went.
The disciple was permitted with Jesus,
Into the courtyard to learn Jesus' fate;
Peter wasn't allowed—
And he waited outside the gate.

(15) The disciple spoke to the girl watching,
To 'Open the gate and let Peter inside;'
She questioned Peter of who he was,
And knowing Jesus, Peter denied!
Peter joined the soldiers and servants
Around a fire for it was cold,

(19) Inside the house, Jesus was questioned,
By the High Priest, of what He told.
Jesus answered, *What I say is widely known.*
For in many temples I did preach,
I've said nothing in private,
That in public I did not teach.

Ask the ones who have heard me speak,

There are some here in our midst.

One of the soldiers standing there

Struck Jesus with his fist!

"Is that the way to answer

The High Priest?" he demanded,

If I have lied, prove it! said Jesus,

I tell the truth as He commanded.

(24) Then Annias sent Jesus

To the High Priest, Caiaphas, for trial.

Meanwhile, Peter was questioned again,

Of knowing Jesus he renewed his denial.

Just then a slave stepped forward asking;

"Weren't you in the olive grove?"

"NO!" said Peter, a third time,

(27) Just then a rooster crowed . . .

Jesus' trial, in front of Caiaphas,

Ended in early dawn.

Next He was taken to the Roman governor,

"Pilate," as he was known.

Pilate came out at the mob's request,
For the Jews were not allowed
To enter the house of a Gentile
And Pilate addressed the crowd;
(29) "What are your charges against this man?"
"He is guilty," they cried,
"Take Him away and judge Him yourself!"
"But we want Him crucified!"
Pilate's approval was needed for that.
And back into the palace he went.
He commanded Jesus be brought to him,
(For they wouldn't let him relent).
He questioned Jesus before him,
(33) "Are You the King of the Jews?"
Jesus answered with a question . . .
How is the word "KING" used?
"Am I a Jew?" Pilate retorted,
"Your own people have brought you in;
Answer my question, what have you done,
And are you truly a king?"

(36) *I am not what you call 'king'*, said Jesus,
My kingdom is not of this earth.
"But you are a king," Pilate replied,
Jesus answered, *Yes, 'twas the purpose of my birth.*
I came to bring truth into the world,
And all who love truth follow me.

(38) "What is truth?!" Pilate exclaimed,
And there was no guilt, Pilate could see.
So he went to the people and told them,
"Jesus is not guilty of any crime;
And you have a custom of asking me,
To release a prisoner at Passover time.
I shall release the 'King of the Jews'."

(40) "No! Release Barabbas," they cried.
(Barabbas was a murderer and thief.)
Then Pilate went back inside.

Chapter XIX

(1) Then Pilate laid open Jesus' back,
Using a whip beaded with lead;
The soldiers made a crown of thorns,
And placed it on His head.
"Hail, King of the Jews!" they mocked,
And struck Him with their fists.
Pilate went outside again, and told them,
"Clearly understand this:
(4) I find Him not guilty!"
Then Jesus came out adorned;
With a purple robe upon His back,
And on His head a crown of thorns.
At the sight of Him, the crowd went wild,
Shouting, "Crucify! Crucify! Crucify!"
"You crucify Him," Pilate said,
"You found Him guilty, not I."

"He calls Himself the Son of God,
For this, He should die, by our law!"
(8) When Pilate heard this he was more frightened than ever,
(Was there something more than he saw?)
Back into the palace he went with Jesus,
"Now tell me where you are from."
Jesus didn't reply, only looked at him,
(10) At this—Pilate came undone!
"You won't talk to me or answer my questions,
I have great power, don't you know?
I can have you crucified,
And I have the power to let you go!"
You would have no power over me,
Unless it were given from on High;
And those who have the greater sin, said Jesus,
Are the ones who want me to die.
Then, Pilate went out, and tried to release Him again,
But the Jewish leaders intervened;
"No!" they warned Pilate, "He is a rebel,
If He declares Himself to be King!"

(13) At these words Pilate sent for Jesus,
To be brought to 'the pavement' outside;
"Here is your King!" Pilate said to the Jews,
And they shouted, "We want Him crucified!"
"What?" answered Pilate. "Crucify your King?"
The time was about noon before Passover day;
"We have no king but Caesar!" they cried,
(16) And Pilate gave them Jesus, to have their way.
They placed a cross upon His back,
And marched Him from the city to a hill;
The place was called Golgotha,
And there Jesus obeyed God's will.

(18) They crucified Jesus with two others,
And high on this cross for people to view;
Pilate posted a sign that read,
"Jesus of Nazareth, King of the Jews."
Then the chief priests said to Pilate,
"Change it so it will read;
'He said I am King of the Jews,'"
But Pilate would not heed.

"What I have written, I have written,
It stays as it is," they heard Pilate speak;
(20) The sign was in three languages:
Latin, Hebrew, and Greek.
(23) The soldiers divided Jesus' clothes,
And cast lots for His robe;
Doing this fulfilled the prophecy,
From Psalm 22:18 that was foretold.
From the cross, Jesus gazed down,
(26) He saw His Mother, as she was stunned;
His close friend was there beside her,
Jesus said, *He is your son.*
And she is your Mother.
Are the words He said to me;
(27) Then I took her to my home,
In my care she would always be.
Jesus knew now that everything was finished,
And as He lowered His head;
He murmured, *I am thirsty,*
Fulfilling what the scriptures said.

(29) A jug of sour wine was there,
They used a sponge to dip;
They tied this on a hyssop branch,
And held it to His lips.
When Jesus had tasted this,
These final words He said;
(30) *It is finished.* And dismissed His spirit,
As He bowed His head.
The next day was the Sabbath,
And Passover observance, too;
The Jewish leaders agreed,
And knew what they must do.
They spoke to Pilate to hasten the death
Of those being crucified;
For they didn't want them hanging there,
As visitors travel by.
So the soldiers came and broke the legs,
Of the men hanging at Jesus' side;
They didn't need to do this for Jesus,
For He had already died.

(34) Yet one of the soldiers reached up,
And pierced Jesus with his spear;
Blood and water flowed from His side,
I saw, for I was standing near.
Joseph of Arimathea,
A secret disciple so bold;
Asked Pilate for Jesus' body,
"Take it!" he was told.
With the help of Nicodemus,
They carefully took Jesus away;
They rubbed Him with ointment, and wrapped His body,
As was the custom of the day.
There was a new tomb in a garden,
Not far from the crucifixion place;
The Sabbath was drawing near,
They laid Him there in haste.

Chapter XX

(1) Early Sunday morning,
As darkness turned to dawn;
Mary Magdalene came to the tomb,
And found Jesus gone!
In desperation she ran,
And found Simon Peter and me;
We hurried to the tomb,
To see what we could see!
I outran Peter and got there first,
(5) Stooped, and looked inside;
The linen cloth was lying there,
Jesus was wrapped in after He died.
Then Simon Peter arrived,
I followed, as he entered in;
Only the swath of cloth was there,
—We gazed at where Jesus had been.

(8) I saw, and I believed,
That Jesus had risen from the dead;
For until that moment—
We hadn't realized what the scriptures said.
Peter and I went on home,
But Mary returned to the tomb;
She was standing there weeping,
Then stooped to look into the little room.

(12) She saw two white-robed angels,
Sitting where Jesus had lain;
"Why are you crying?" the angels asked,
And Mary tried to explain.
"They have taken away my Lord,
And I don't know where He can be!"

(14) Instantly Jesus appeared behind her,
And she didn't know it was He;

(15) *Why are you crying*? Jesus asked her,
And whom are you looking for?
Thinking He was the gardener,
She thought she could find out more.

"Sir, tell me where you have put Him,
If you have taken Him away;
I will go and get Him."
Then she heard Jesus say,

(16) *Mary*! and she turned to Him,
"Teacher!" she exclaimed.
She realized it was Jesus,
The instant He spoke her name.
Do not touch Me, He cautioned,
For I have not yet ascended;
Go and tell my brothers,
I go to our Father, He commanded.

(18) Mary Magdalene went at once,
To give the disciples the word;
"I have seen the Lord," she exclaimed,
They were amazed at what they heard.

(19) That evening the disciples,
Met in secret behind locked doors;
For fear the Jewish leaders,
Would trouble them some more.

Suddenly, Jesus appeared in their midst,
How wonderful was their joy;
He greeted them and showed His wounds,
And gave them this employ—
(21) *As My Father has sent me,*
So send I you;
Then, Jesus breathed on them,
And told them what they must do.
Receive the Holy Spirit,
And if you forgive anyone's sins;
They will be forgiven,
And Jesus disappeared again.
(24) One of the disciples named Thomas,
Was not with them at the time;
They tried to tell him what had occurred,
But Thomas wanted to see the signs.
I must touch the wounds in His hands
And put my hand in His side;
Then I'll believe He has returned,"
This was Thomas' reply.

(26) Eight days later the disciples gathered,
Behind locked doors for a meeting;
Suddenly Jesus was in their midst . . .
Giving them greeting.
Then He said to Thomas,
Touch the wounds in my hands and side;
Don't be faithless any longer, believe!
Then—Thomas cried—
"My Lord and my God!"
And Jesus continued to say;
(29) *You believe because you've seen Me,*
Standing here today.
But blessed are those who haven't seen Me,
And believe on Me just the same;
But Jesus' disciples saw other miracles,
Than these recorded in His name.
Jesus is God's Son, the Messiah,
These things are written to believe;
Do this, and eternal life,
Will be yours to receive.

Chapter XXI

(1) Later Jesus appeared again,
By the Lake of Galilee;
To Peter, Thomas, Nathanael, and James,
Two other disciples and me.
Peter said, "I'm going fishing,"
And we decided to go along;
We fished all night, catching nothing,
'Till the early dawn.

(4) We saw a man standing on the beach,
But who he was we couldn't see;
He called to us and told us,
Where the fish would be.
Cast your nets to the right of the boat,
We did as we were told;
The fish were so many and the weight so heavy,
The net would hardly hold.

(7) "It is the Lord!" I said to Peter,
Then Peter jumped in and swam ashore;
The rest of us stayed in the boat,
And to the beach, the loaded net we bore.
When we arrived, we saw a fire,
And fish in a pan, were beginning to fry;
With it was some bread,
And Jesus said, as He was standing by,
(10) *Bring some fish you've caught*,
Peter dragged the net ashore that morn;
His count was one hundred, fifty-three large fish,
Yet, the net hadn't torn.
Now come and have some breakfast, said Jesus,
Then He served us fish and bread;
This was the third time He had appeared to us,
Since His return from the dead.
(15) After breakfast Jesus said to Peter,
"Do you love me more than these?"
"Yes, You know I am your friend,"
Peter replied with ease.

Then feed my Lambs, said Jesus,

And He questioned Peter again;

Son of John, do you really love me?

"Yes, Lord, You know I am your friend."

Then take care of my Sheep, said Jesus.

Yet—He asked Peter once more;

Simon, are you even my friend?

And Peter answered as before.

"Lord, You know I am,

For you know my heart."

Peter was grieved at the way Jesus asked,

(17) The same question in three parts.

Then Jesus challenged Peter again,

—Feed My Sheep.

And Peter listened to his Lord,

So every word would keep.

When you were young, said Jesus,

You were able to do as you liked;

But when you are old, you will stretch out your hands,

And others will direct your life.

(19) Jesus said these things, to let Peter know,
What kind of death his would be;
Peter would die to glorify God,
Then Jesus told him, *Follow Me.*
Peter looked around and saw,
John, the disciple Jesus loved;
"What sort of death will he die?" said Peter,
Then was answered by our Lord from above.

(23) *If I want him to live until I return,*
What is that to you?
"I am the disciple, John,
I know these things are true.
And I suppose if all the events,
In Jesus' life were reported;
The world could hardly contain the books,
If His deeds were all recorded."

About the Author

"Anything is possible if a person believes."

Mark 9:23

The things that are impossible with people are surely possible with God, and I am living proof of that. This book is proof that He can do anything with a lump of clay – This one called Dottie Reed – yet this book is not about me, it is about Him, Jesus Christ!

To Him be the glory what's taken from His Word!

My name is Dottie Reed and I'm here to attest, I'm amazed at how I believe God is using me to share His Word. I have no college degrees to add after my name, but I'm finding that might not be completely needed; beneficial of course, but it's hard to explain. God tells us, as I think of it, through His Holy Word, we need Him the most. We try Him first, last and all in between and see what happens!

It took me quite a while to find this out. My parents were the best! They loved the six of us children, they gave us the necessities of life...sometimes month to month! We all worked hard, and laughed, loved and helped each other in so many ways. How so thankful am I to have been born into the Mitchell family at Duncan, Mississippi!

We grew up going to church, I gave my heart to Jesus at age 11....married just after graduation, to high school sweetheart, Joe Wayne Reed at age 17. I became a mother at age 20 of a beautiful little girl, we named Lori, 5 yrs. later a little boy, Joe W. Reed, Jr.....Time passed so fast, ups and downs all in between. We still went to church, but that was about it.

Then after 30 or so years, I realized with all the "things" we'd done and accomplished, a successful construction business, home, children....yet nothing was completely satisfying. Then one night at age 47, I realized God was who I needed. I had known Him for years and years, but hadn't lived for Him. The night I gave my repentance, I shall never forget the peace that came over me.

The next morning, early, with coffee, I opened my Bible to the Gospel of John. I had heard from some pastor that this was the best chapter in which to start for a "new" Christian.

From there, I started to journal my prayers, for family and all that was on my mind. I'd always liked to write rhymes from an early age, now the scriptures seem to tell a story in rhyme. My prayer was to not change the meaning of anything, because I remembered Revelation 22:18-19! Two and one half years later, this writing was finished. I loved doing it, but didn't know what to do WITH it! I put it in a drawer, getting it out from time to time.

Then I taught Sunday School and Children's church, through which I was inspired to create a couple of children's books, "JONAH" and "BARTIMAEUS". I am currently praying God will show me how to bring these illustrated children's stories to life.

And now, with the kind encouragement of family and friends, I have found an avenue to share this labor of love. I continue to journal my prayers and devotionals every morning. My life is filled with His blessings of family, joy and love. May all praise be directed to Him who is our "All in All."

"Let every thing that hath breath praise the Lord. Praise ye the Lord."

Psalm 150:6

READER'S NOTES

READER'S NOTES

READER'S NOTES

READER'S NOTES

READER'S NOTES

READER'S NOTES